Easy Christmas
Instrumental Solos

CONTENTS

Arranged by Bill Galliford, Ethan Neuburg and Tod Edmondson

© 2009 Alfred Mu...
All Rights Res...

ISBN-10: 0-7390-6226-3
ISBN-13: 978-0-7390-6226-5

Track 1: Demo

BELIEVE
(from *The Polar Express*)

Words and Music by
ALAN SILVESTRI
and GLENN BALLARD

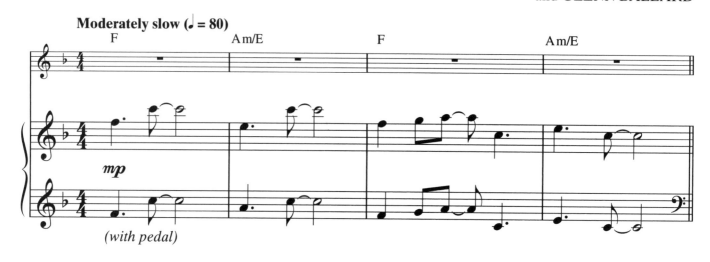

Track 2: Demo

DECK THE HALL

Traditional

DANCE OF THE SUGAR-PLUM FAIRY

(from *The Nutcracker Suite*)

By PETER ILYICH TCHAIKOVSKY

Track 3: Demo

Moderately slow (♩ = 112)

Dance of the Sugar-Plum Fairy - 2 - 1
33292

THE FIRST NOËL

Track 4: Demo

Traditional

FELIZ NAVIDAD

Track 5: Demo

Words and Music by
JOSÉ FELICIANO

Feliz Navidad - 3 - 1
33292

FROSTY THE SNOWMAN

Words and Music by
STEVE NELSON and JACK ROLLINS

Frosty the Snowman - 3 - 1
33292

Frosty the Snowman - 3 - 3
33292

HARK! THE HERALD ANGELS SING

Track 7: Demo

Music by
FELIX MENDELSSOHN

Track 8: Demo

JINGLE BELL ROCK

Words and Music by
JOE BEAL and JIM BOOTHE

Jingle Bell Rock - 3 - 1
33292

Track 9: Demo

JINGLE BELLS

By J. PIERPONT

Moderately fast (♩ = 144)
(♩ = 72 This represents the song pulse feel counted in two.)

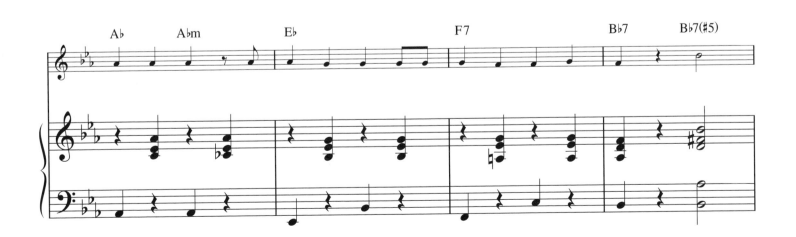

JINGLE BELL ROCK

Track 8: Demo

Words and Music by
JOE BEAL and JIM BOOTHE

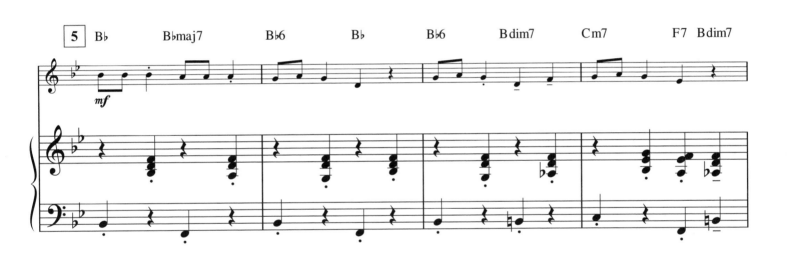

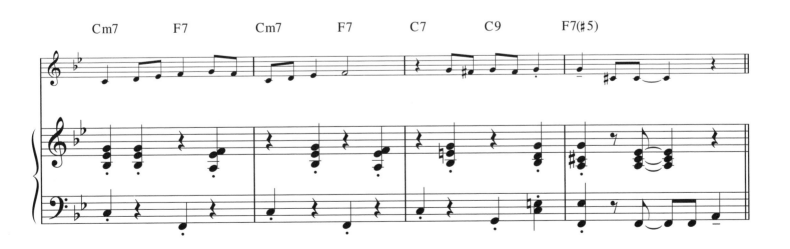

Jingle Bell Rock - 3 - 1
33292

LET IT SNOW! LET IT SNOW! LET IT SNOW!

Track 10: Demo

Music by
JULE STYNE

Let It Snow! Let It Snow! Let It Snow! - 3 - 1
33292

THE LITTLE DRUMMER BOY

Words and Music by
HARRY SIMEONE, HENRY ONORATI
and **KATHERINE DAVIS**

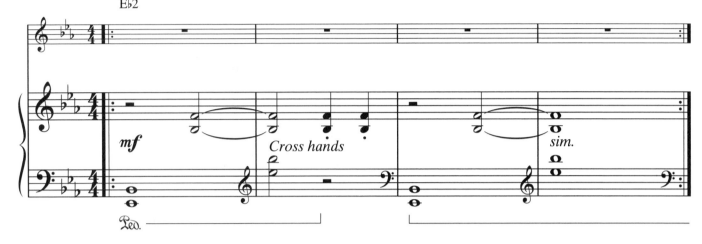

The Little Drummer Boy - 3 - 1
33292

A little slower (♩ = 60)

Track 12: Demo

SILENT NIGHT

Words and Music by
JOSEPH MOHR and FRANZ GRUBER

Moderately ♩ = 116

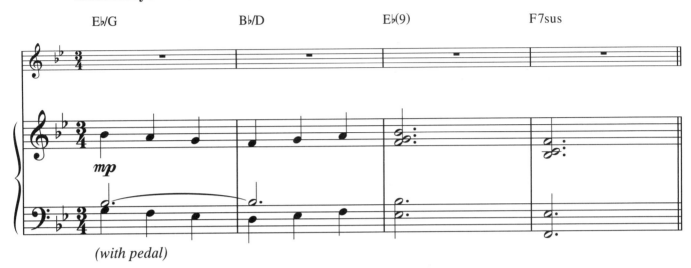

(with pedal)

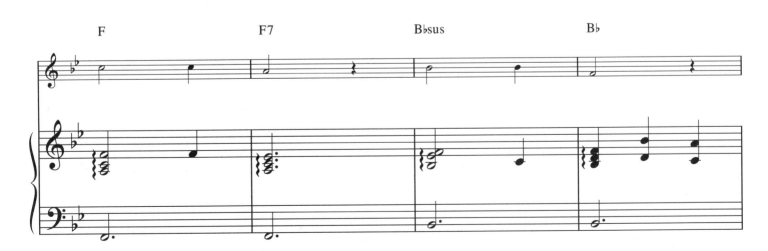

Silent Night - 4 - 1
33292

Track 13: Demo

SLEIGH RIDE

By LEROY ANDERSON

Moderately bright, with spirit (♩ = 184)
(♩ = 92 This represents the song pulse feel counted in two.)

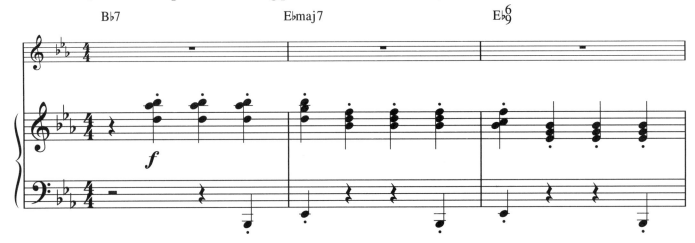

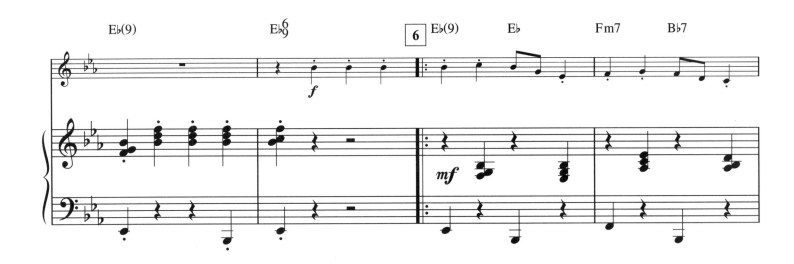

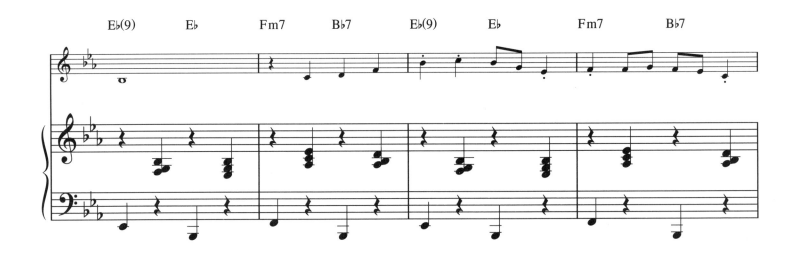

Sleigh Ride - 4 - 1
33292

YOU'RE A MEAN ONE, MR. GRINCH

(from Dr. Seuss' *How The Grinch Stole Christmas*)

Track 14: Demo

Music by
ALBERT HAGUE

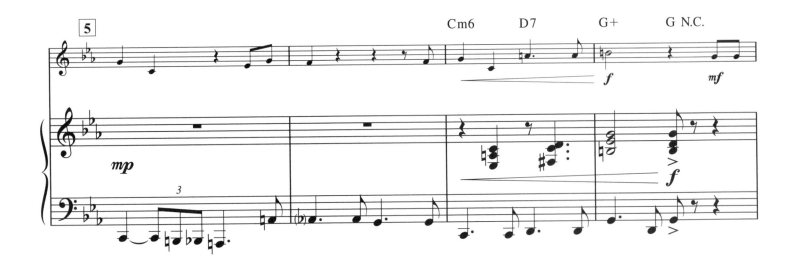

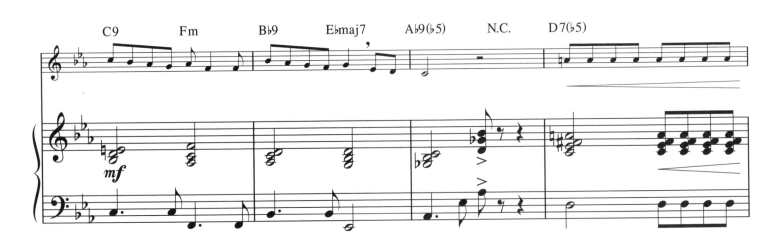

You're a Mean One, Mr. Grinch - 3 - 1
33292